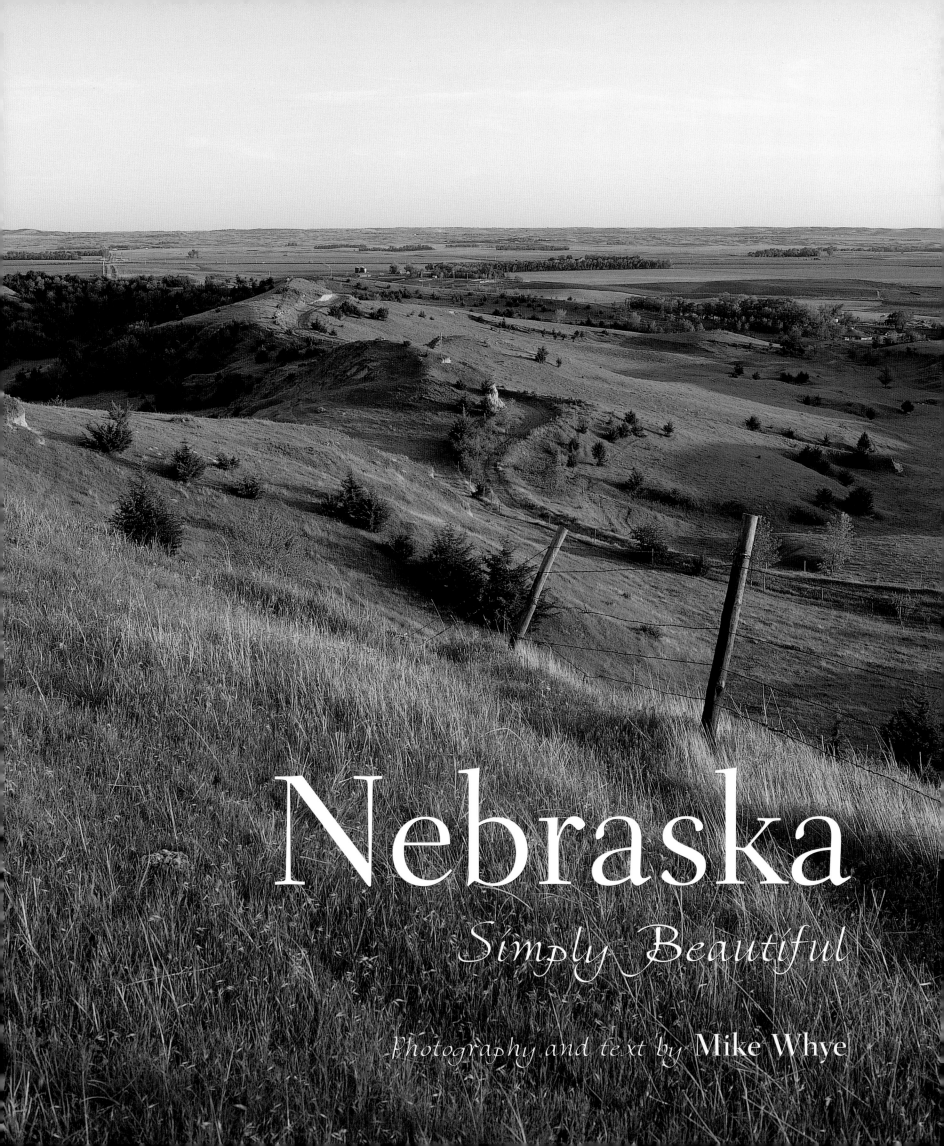

Nebraska
Simply Beautiful

Photography and text by **Mike Whye**

THIS BOOK IS DEDICATED TO MY FATHER,
WHO HELPED FORM MY INTEREST IN
PHOTOGRAPHY, AND TO MY MOTHER, WHO
TAUGHT ME HOW TO VIEW LIFE AS ART.

TITLE PAGE: *A spur of the Sandhills overlooks the plains south of Merna. An ancient seabed millions of years ago, the low-lying Sandhills cover one-quarter of the state, making them Nebraska's largest geological feature.*

RIGHT: *The Missouri River between Nebraska (foreground) and South Dakota rolls near its confluence with the Niobrara River. Not channeled like portions of the river below Sioux City, the Missouri here still has a wealth of backwaters, islands, and sandbars.*

FRONT COVER: *The red leaves of sumac create accent marks on the prairie in the Sandhills east of Thedford.*

BACK COVER: *Water tumbles down a sandstone cliff at Smith Falls, east of Valentine.*

FLAP PHOTO: *Western boots top a row of fenceposts in the Sandhills near Anselmo.*

PAGE 4: *Prickly stems guard the delicate blossoms of an evening primrose. Often found along roads in western Nebraska and the Sandhills, such as this one near Thedford, evening primroses flower in June and July.*

PAGE 5: *Grassy prairie gives way to tortured terrain eroded by rain and wind at Chimney Rock near Bayard. Written about more than any other landmark by those who traveled the Oregon Trail in the nineteenth century, Chimney Rock measures about 325 feet from its base to the tip of its spire.*

ISBN 1-56037-311-3
Photography © 2004 by Mike Whye
© 2004 Farcountry Press

For more information about our books write Farcountry Press, P.O. Box 5630, Helena, MT 59604; call (800) 821-3874; or visit www.farcountrypress.com.

Created, produced, and designed in the United States.
Printed in China.

INTRODUCTION BY MIKE WHYE

I first experienced Nebraska when I was 15 and had just moved from the east coast; my father, who was in the Air Force, had been transferred to Offutt Air Force Base in Bellevue. Just a few miles from our home in town were big, wide, open fields that seemed to stretch forever under skies that did the same.

A few months after we arrived, some friends drove me to Lincoln, and on the way there I saw land that was even bigger, wider, and more open than that near Bellevue. Every time we crested a hill, those open spaces grew. This certainly was not like what I had known in New England.

That fall I camped alongside the Platte River with some other kids from a church group. I couldn't believe the Platte—it was wide, like some other rivers I had seen, but so shallow that my friends and I could walk almost all the way across it on sandbars, the water no higher than our waists.

The more I traveled in Nebraska, the more I appreciated what I saw in this land where the horizon appears endless and lies low. Some call it flat. In a few places, such as along the valley floors flanking various rivers, that's true but, overall, Nebraska is not flat. Instead, its rolling hills give it the character of an ocean where the waves are wide. Those who traveled West in the mid-nineteenth century on the Oregon, California, and Mormon Pioneer Trails apparently felt that way, too, calling their white canvas-topped wagons "prairie schooners," which must have looked like sailing ships on the wide, sea-like prairie. Surely in those days, and the countless days prior, when the wind blew grasses that then ruled the prairie, it must have looked just as Nebraska author Willa Cather describes it in *My Antonia:* "...there was so much motion in it; the whole country seemed, somehow, to be running."

The landscape of Nebraska is surprisingly varied. In the eastern part of the state, trees heavy with leaves shade such places as the hollows of Fontenelle Forest, where, so to speak, I cut my teeth in nature photography. Western Nebraska, however, is radically different, the land ruggedly beautiful. The high plains of the Oglala National Grassland bask in the golden sun. And the Agate Fossil Beds, while they appear forsaken of everything, possess a unique beauty. In some cases, Nebraska's splendors are tucked away where you would not expect to find them. That's the case in the northern Sandhills when you come upon the Niobrara River near Valentine. The transition is sudden from sky-capped plains to a deeply cut valley where about 200 waterfalls, large and small, drop spring-fed waters into a shallow clear river lined with meadows and rocky, pine-filled canyons.

Contrasting with Nebraska's natural glories are its manmade treasures. In downtown Omaha the First National Tower, the tallest building between Chicago and Denver, touches the sky in elegance. In areas where little more than grass grew for centuries, irrigation systems slowly revolve as they water corn and soybeans, giving new meaning to the term "crop circles." In North Platte, one of the largest locomotives ever made stands as a striking and powerful tribute to when steam drove much of our nation. Even in the remote areas of the Sandhills, humanity's influence is seen in the form of thin, spindly windmills, quietly turning in the prairie breeze, drawing water up from the world's largest aquifer to splash into the metal tanks for livestock to drink.

As for the Nebraskans, they are as varied as the landforms, yet all combine their cultures to create the Nebraska spirit. Some reflect upon the ancient heritage that still flows through their veins by occasionally wearing clothing similar to what their grandfathers and grandmothers wore in other countries. Others celebrate traditions such as raising the flag each morning. And then some just enjoy being, even if that means doing nothing more than dabbling their toes in the cool water of a small pond in the morning sunlight.

With all that Nebraska has to offer, I feel sorry for those who just whiz through the state on Interstate 80; they lose so much by not getting off the main route. In a way, Nebraska is a sleeper; that is, it does not have the dramatic mountains and the raging seacoasts that immediately bowl you backwards. Instead, its beauty is more subtle. It comes in the form of watching a cowboy turn his horse in the red dust of a late afternoon. Or in discovering a family of baby rabbits nestled together as you walk across your backyard. Or in listening to the cacophony of sandhill cranes calling to each other as they settle into the waters of the Platte in the fading light of a March evening.

I hope that my photographs impart a sense of the beauty that exists in Nebraska, and I encourage people to travel this state and to take their time doing so. It truly is simply beautiful.

LEFT: *Canoeists on the Niobrara River pass by looming cliffs at Fort Niobrara National Wildlife Refuge. Favored by paddlers from across the nation for its shallow and clear waters, the Niobrara passes through elements of six ecosystems in this part of its valley northeast of Valentine.*

FACING PAGE: *Farm fields appear as art, near Humboldt.* LARRY MAYER

A cowboy turns his horse in the dust of a late afternoon, Fort Robinson State Park.

A hazy sky creates a golden sunset over the Sandhills east of Burwell. Covering more than 19,600 square miles, the Sandhills are the largest set of sand dunes in the western hemisphere.

ABOVE: *Typical of some scenes in central and western Nebraska, a sign announcing the entrance to a ranch where no other structures can be seen hangs above a county road northwest of Hay Springs.*

LEFT: *Originally given the Oto name Nebraska, meaning "flat water," the Platte River traverses the entire state from east to west. Considered by some to be too thin to plow and too thick to drink, the wide, shallow river served as the watery lifeline for thousands who traveled the Oregon, Mormon Pioneer, and California Trails that paralleled the Platte across much of the state.*

With bare and deeply cut ravines and crevices, the arid landscape of Toadstool Park northwest of Crawford more closely resembles Mars than Nebraska. Researchers have found traces of animals that lived here about 30 million years ago, when this region was a wetland.

LARRY MAYER

RIGHT: From 1892 to 1968, flour and feed were milled at Champion Mill, which stands alongside the waters of Frenchman Creek at Champion. The mill was the last water-powered mill in Nebraska before becoming a state historical park in 1969.

BELOW: Made of automobile parts, a dinosaur stands watch over Carhenge on the east side of Alliance. During a 1987 family reunion, engineering consultant James Reinders and about three dozen of his relatives painted 38 automobiles gray and placed them in a pattern resembling the stones at England's Stonehenge, built about 3,000 years earlier.

Pines spot and line portions of the Sandhills in the Bessey Ranger District of the Nebraska National Forest west of Halsey. Beginning in 1902, millions of pines were planted here under the direction of the University of Nebraska. Today the 90,444-acre preserve contains 20,000 acres of trees, the largest manmade forest in the nation, and produces seedlings for use in Nebraska, Kansas, Wyoming, Colorado, and South Dakota.

RIGHT: *After a day of feeding in the fields alongside the Platte River near Kearney, sandhill cranes pepper the western sky as they return to the river on a spring evening. Each night they sleep while standing in the river's shallow waters, which offer protection from predators such as coyote and fox.*

BELOW: *Pumpkins almost overrun a produce store and its grounds in west Omaha. This part of the city comprised fields and farms until the sprawl of residential and commercial developments overtook them, making this store one of the last of its kind in the area.*

Walls, roofs, eaves, and dormers create a collection of angles at Neligh Mill State Historical Park in Neligh. Built in stages beginning in 1873, the mill remained in business for 96 years alongside the Elkhorn River.

RIGHT: *Residents proud of their Czech heritage prepare to strike up the band in front of the Wilber Hotel in Wilber. Settled heavily by Czech immigrants in the 1850s and 1860s, Wilber calls itself the Czech Capital of Nebraska and celebrates that honor with a festival the first full weekend in August.*

BELOW: *Two young visitors peer at the wide parade grounds at Fort Hartsuff State Historical Park. Built in 1874 between Burwell and Ord, the fort was used by the Army only until 1881. Besides serving as a military post, the fort was the region's social center and marketplace.*

The North Loup River
wends its way through a
wintry landscape at sunset.
LARRY MAYER

An elk wanders a meadow at Wildcat Hills State Recreation Area south of Gering. Buffalo and deer also make their home on the preserve, which is located in a range of hills that line the south side of the North Platte River in the panhandle.

Nourished by the waters of the Snake River, grasses, bushes, and trees grow thick along the riverbanks, creating an oasis in otherwise arid Cherry County southwest of Valentine.

ABOVE: *Wheat flour made by this mill machinery at Neligh Mill Historical Park was sent to many places in the U.S. and England during the mill's early years.*

FACING PAGE: *Haybales lie in the Platte River valley northwest of Cozad.*

ABOVE: Recalling a time when steamboats were the main form of transportation along Nebraska's eastern flank, the Spirit of Brownville takes visitors for a ride on the Missouri River near Brownville, considered Nebraska's oldest community.

LEFT: Small weathered pines cling to a hardscrabble existence atop a bluff in Smiley Canyon, a part of Fort Robinson State Park. Almost a mile above sea level, this portion of the state is considerably drier than places in eastern Nebraska.

ABOVE: *A center-point irrigation system stretches across a wheat field, providing much-needed water to the growing crops. Approximately eight million acres of fields in Nebraska are irrigated.* MICHAEL FORSBERG

FACING PAGE: *Belying the notion that all of Nebraska is flat, a series of gullies and breaks add drama to the landscape near Lexington.* LARRY MAYER

RIGHT: *Boatsmate Third Class Jose Chavez, who just became a U.S. citizen, raises the flag on the U.S. Coast Guard Cutter Gasconade before it leaves its port north of Omaha. Every spring the crew places navigation buoys on the Missouri River; they maintain the shore stations and then recover the buoys in the fall, at the end of the navigation season.*

BELOW: *Lights begin to glow in the early evening at the Bar 99 Ranch north of Merriman. Started in 1894 by Arthur Bowring, who was the first to settle on this land in the northern Sandhills, the ranch was also the home of his second wife, Eva Bowring, Nebraska's first and thus far only female U.S. senator. She was appointed by the Nebraska governor to complete the term of Dwight Griswold, who had died in 1954. The 7,200-acre spread is now the Arthur Bowring Sandhills Ranch State Historical Park and remains a working ranch.*

FACING PAGE: *The Gene Leahy Mall in Omaha takes on a different character as evening falls and the lights of the various downtown buildings begin to glow. The long waterway flowing through the mall symbolizes the city's relationship with the Missouri River.*

South of Cozad, rolled bales of hay lie on fields that seem to go on forever under a sky that does likewise. More commonly used now than the rectangular hay bale, a round one can weigh between 750 to 1,500 pounds.

RIGHT; A researcher makes notes while kneeling among the fossilized remains of barrel-chested rhinos at Ash Fall Fossil Beds State Historical Park in Antelope County. About ten million years ago, the rhinos and other animals in this area were suffocated when a blanket of volcanic ash fell upon them.

BELOW: Lifelike statues created by Omaha artist John Lajba portray a scene in the Durham Western Heritage Museum in Omaha. Located in the former Union Depot, which was built by Union Pacific Railroad, the museum's majestic main lobby remains as it was when passenger trains were in their heyday. The museum also has VIP passenger cars used by Union Pacific, as well as various collections and displays related to the history of Omaha.

FACING PAGE: The sun sets over the main channel of the Platte River south of Grand Island.

ABOVE: *Sandhill cranes take to wing near the Platte River. After wintering along the Gulf of Mexico, the cranes congregate on sections of the Platte—particularly between Kearney and Grand Island. They come here each spring to fatten up for their next northbound flights that take some to the far reaches of Canada and Siberia.* MICHAEL FORSBERG

LEFT: *Morning fog rises off the waters of the Missouri River and fields north of Decatur.* LARRY MAYER

ABOVE: *An isolated homestead south of Chadron.* LARRY MAYER

FACING PAGE: *Accompanied by a dusting of snow, thin layers of ice form on channels of the Missouri River near Niobrara State Park. Before a series of dams was built much farther upriver, the Missouri was prone to change its course every so often, especially when swollen with snowmelt from as far away as the Rocky Mountains.*

Given a soft-blue hue by approaching storm clouds, the Niobrara River flows amid prairie grass and trees just beginning to show their fall colors southwest of Valentine.

LEFT: *A young buffalo checks out its grassy surroundings at Fort Niobrara National Wildlife Refuge east of Valentine. Besides about 350 buffalo that live there, the 19,131-acre preserve is home to prairie dogs, elk, deer, and more than 230 types of birds.*

BELOW: *Near the eastern limits of the Sandhills, the stark remains of a lonely tree watch over the stark spaces southwest of Bartlett.*

ABOVE: *A covered wagon overlooks a part of the Oregon Trail at Rock Creek Station State Historical Park east of Fairbury. It is estimated that between 300,000 and 500,000 people traveled the Oregon Trail from 1840 until the railroad finally crossed the nation in the 1860s.*

LEFT: *Storms clouds brew in the distance while sunlight bakes the rocky landscape at Agate Fossil Beds National Monument in Sioux County. In the late nineteenth and early twentieth centuries, paleontologists from around the world came here to study and collect fossils up to 20 million years old.*

ABOVE: *A trio of children climbs up for a ringside view of cowboys and cowgirls warming up for a rodeo held on the grounds of Fort Robinson State Park. Although remote from Nebraska's populated areas, for many years Fort Robinson was the state's most visited state park.*

FACING PAGE: *Clouds and water reflect the warm glow of day's end over a section of the Platte River west of Valley. A major tributary of the Missouri River, the Platte measures nearly 1,000 miles from its sources in the Rocky Mountains to its confluence with the Missouri near Plattsmouth.*

RIGHT: *The modern architecture of an office building in downtown Omaha mirrors the summer sky, almost giving the building a see-through appearance.*

BELOW: *For more than a week each June, the top collegiate baseball players from across the nation come to play in the College World Series at Rosenblatt Stadium in Omaha. Although the championship series began in Michigan in 1947, it has been held in Nebraska since 1950.*

FACING PAGE: *Fall colors begin to tinge a view of the Missouri River and its valley south of Indian Cave State Park.*

ABOVE: *Hay bales lie near a lake amid the northern Sandhills near Merriman.*

FACING PAGE: *Designed by Bertram Goodhue and completed in 1932 after ten years of construction, the Nebraska capitol is the third building in Lincoln to house the offices and chambers of the governor, unicameral legislature, and supreme court justices. The capitol's 400-foot-tall tower is topped by a 19-foot-tall statue of a farmer sowing grain.*

Located in Smith Falls State Park at the end of a sandstone canyon on the south side of the Niobrara River is Smith Falls, Nebraska's tallest waterfall at 75 feet in height.

LEFT: *Two youngsters cool their feet in the waters of Farmers Lake, located in the loess hills east of Wellfleet.*

BELOW: *Silos, storage bins, and a grain elevator rise behind rows of crops east of Grand Island. Crops cover more than 22 million acres in Nebraska, which has a total land area of 49.2 million acres.*

While windmills (above) represent the old tried-and-true system of supplying water to livestock throughout the state, center-point irrigation systems (left) allow crops to be raised in Nebraska's arid regions. Much of the water used for agriculture in the Cornhusker State comes from the Ogallala aquifer, which is estimated to hold more than two billion acre feet of water within Nebraska's borders. LARRY MAYER

ABOVE: *A youngster does his best to cool off a friend on a warm summer day.* KELLY / MOONEY PRODUCTIONS

FACING PAGE: *The sharply etched cliffs and bluffs of the Wildcat Hills (foreground) frame another set of equally rugged hills near Scotts Bluff National Monument, about ten miles away, beyond the flat Cedar Valley.*

The setting sun reveals a bewildering maze of water and land near the upper end of Lewis and Clark Lake, a reservoir formed on the Missouri River by Gavins Point Dam. LARRY MAYER

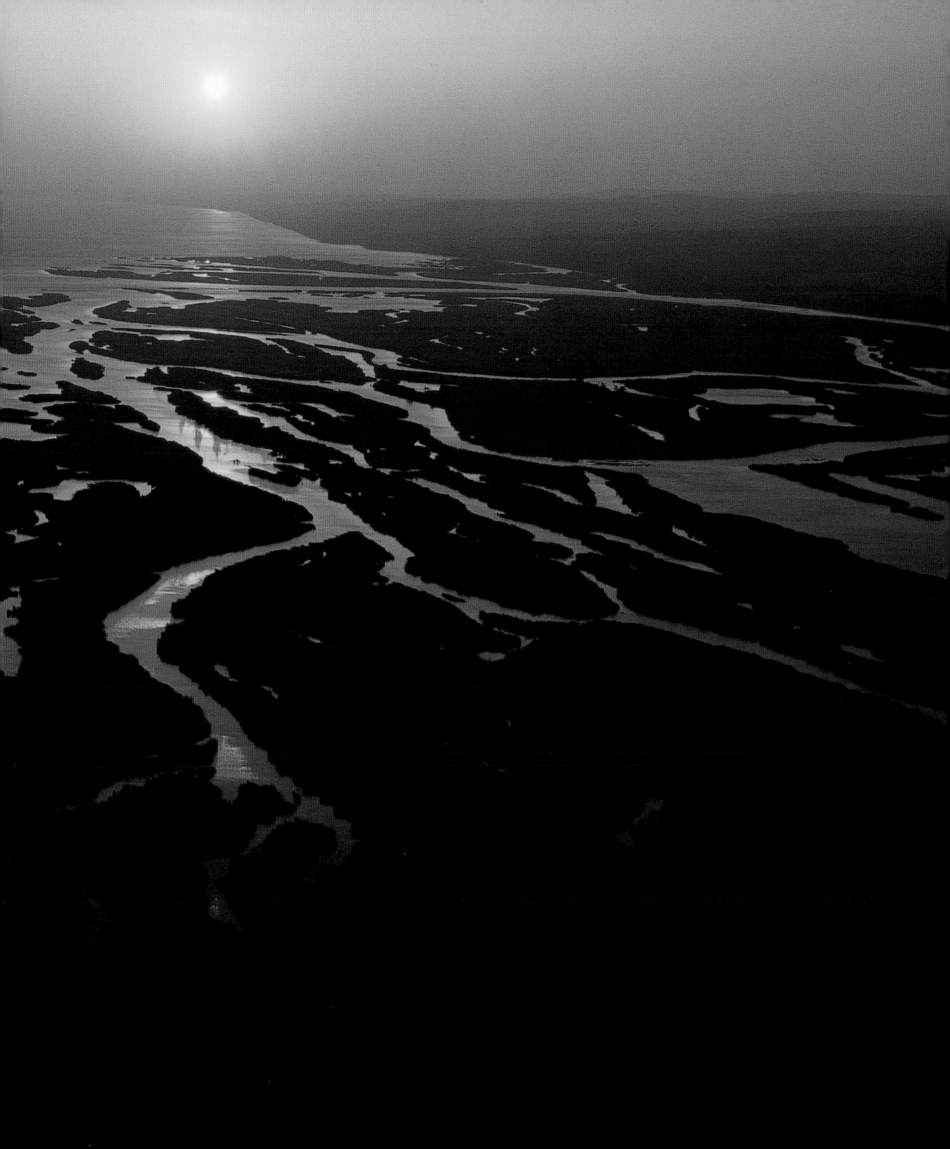

With about half a million people living in its greater metropolitan area, Omaha is the
largest community in Nebraska and on the upper Missouri River. Because the Missouri
was prone to flooding during Omaha's early years, the downtown was built on high
ground away from the river.

LEFT: Named the Spirit of Nebraska, a B-2 bomber sits among patriotic bunting during an annual air show at Offutt Air Force Base in Bellevue. Originally an Army outpost called Ft. Crook, Offutt is the headquarters for the Strategic Command, a joint services unit controlling the nation's nuclear forces.

BELOW: The bust of Native American rights advocate Susette LaFlesche Tibbles (right) heads a line of busts of others who are listed in the Nebraska Hall of Fame and featured in the corridors of the state capitol in Lincoln. Among the others in the Hall of Fame are authors Willa Cather and Mari Sandoz, Chief Standing Bear, scout and showman William F. "Buffalo Bill" Cody, General John "Blackjack" Pershing, and J. Sterling Morton, the founder of Arbor Day.

Located in a rocky canyon amid the arid northern Sandhills, Snake River Falls, southwest of Valentine, are Nebraska's largest by volume.

A small fire burns brightly among artifacts at Dancing Leaf Earth Lodge near *Wellfleet. Built by Les and Jan Hosick, the lodge is a re-creation of those typically built of trees and earth by the Plains Indians. At Dancing Leaf, visitors can learn about Native American cultures and stay overnight in the earth lodge.*

Despite its apparent emptiness, Toadstool Park, in Nebraska's northwest corner, is home to a variety of creatures, including the western hognose snake (left). Erosion at the park continues to slowly sculpt strange shapes (below) out of the rock.

ABOVE: Morning sunlight strikes the architectural splendors of the May Museum in Fremont. The first part of the house was built in 1874 by Caroline and Theron Nye, the town's first mayor. Their son, Ray, added onto the house in the early twentieth century, creating a 25-room Italianate mansion. Years later, the Louis E. May Trust saved the house from demolition and turned it into a museum.

RIGHT: In the broad valley of the Platte River north of Schuyler, a farmer stops along a country road to check his crops.

ABOVE: *A red fox pauses before heading up the forested hillside to its den of hungry pups,*
Fontenelle Forest. MICHAEL FORSBERG

FACING PAGE: *Paled by rain clouds, light from the morning sun silvers the waters of the*
Niobrara River. Beginning in Wyoming's Front Range of the Rocky Mountains, the Niobrara
spends most of its 430-mile journey flowing across northern Nebraska. The name is believed
to be an Omaha word that means "spreading water." LARRY MAYER

LEFT: *Waters from the Niobrara River (foreground) finally meet those of the Missouri in northeast Nebraska. For many years this region was home to the Ponca, who were forced to move to Oklahoma in 1876. In 1879, Standing Bear won a federal lawsuit to return to his homeland, which he and several of his followers then did.*

BELOW: *Built in 1943 for the Union Pacific Railroad, Challenger 3977 is one of the largest steam locomotives ever made and was capable of reaching 80 miles an hour; it now quietly leads the railroad exhibits on display in North Platte's Cody Park. The Union Pacific has had a long history with North Platte, which holds the world's largest train yard, the Bailey Yard, where about 10,000 train cars are sorted every day.*

FACING PAGE: *Prairie grasses wave in the wind on a part of the high plains once traversed by the Sidney-Deadwood Trail in Box Butte County. Before railroads reached western South Dakota, the trail was the main route from the railhead at Sidney to the gold fields in the Black Hills.*

A young visitor pats the nose of a horse at Eugene T. Mahoney State Park on a wintry day. Opened in 1991 and located halfway between Omaha and Lincoln, Mahoney has become a very popular stop on Interstate 80, drawing about a million visitors each year, the most of any park in the state.

RIGHT: *Snow geese blend in with their namesake on a winter day at Pioneers Park in Lincoln.*

BELOW: *A stream curls its way through a lowland forest on part of the Missouri River floodplain in Fontenelle Forest in Bellevue. Bounded by residential developments and the Missouri, the 1,400-acre preserve provides a peaceful oasis for residents of the greater Omaha metro area.*

ABOVE: *Heading west, a lone bicyclist pedals down a long slope of U.S. Highway 136 west of Brownville.*

LEFT: *Light gray against a darker cloud, a wall cloud rotates upward over fields in southwest Garden County. Moments after this picture was taken, a funnel dropped from this formation but did not touch the ground. Another funnel from this system, however, did hit a few buildings on the north side of Ogallala.*

RIGHT: *A bullfrog and its reflection rest in the quiet waters of a marsh in Fontenelle Forest. Years ago, the Missouri River flowed here but, as it did every so often, the river changed its channel and this area became a wetland.*

BELOW: *A sea of sunflowers brighten a field in the Sandhills near Burwell.*

FACING PAGE: *Trees and thick foliage cover the flanks of hills lining a hollow in Fontenelle Forest in Bellevue. It was near here in 1822 that Joshua Pilcher built a trading post that was later taken over by Lucien Fontenelle, a French fur trader, and his son, Logan Fontenelle, who is the namesake of the forest.*

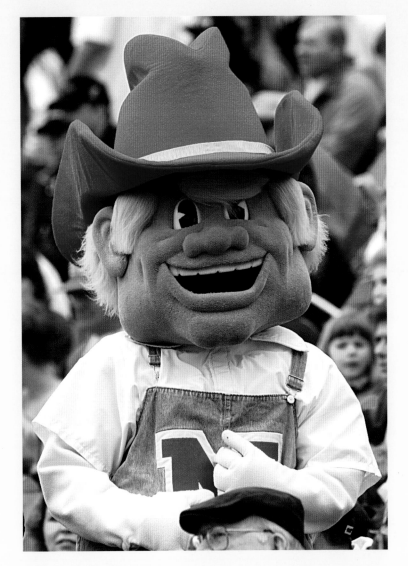

ABOVE: Although Herbie Husker is the nickname of the University of Nebraska's mascot, the athletes are known as the Cornhuskers, a moniker bestowed upon them by a Lincoln sports editor in 1900. Previously they had been called the Antelopes and Bugeaters. LINCOLN JOURNAL STAR

LEFT: On certain Saturdays each autumn when the Cornhusker football team takes to the field, the University of Nebraska's Memorial Stadium (73,918 seats) becomes Nebraska's third largest community. Since November 3, 1962, they have sold out every home game, an NCAA record. LINCOLN JOURNAL STAR

RIGHT: *Baby rabbits huddle in a nest lined by their mother with fur and dry grass in a residential yard in Bellevue.*

BELOW: *A young visitor on a hill at Niobrara State Park looks over the Niobrara River.*

FACING PAGE: *Thin veils of water run down sandstone walls at Fort Falls at Fort Niobrara National Wildlife Refuge. The waterfall is one of about 200 found along the Niobrara River northeast of Valentine where a 76-mile stretch is designated as a National Scenic River.*

LEFT: *A statue of Abraham Lincoln with head bowed stands before a granite engraving of his Gettysburg Address on the west side of the state capitol grounds in Lincoln. Dedicated in 1912, the statue was created by Daniel Chester French, who also made the statue at the Lincoln Memorial in Washington, D.C.*

BELOW: *A small herd of elk wanders on the plains in southern Morrill County in Nebraska's panhandle.*

FACING PAGE: *Fall colors fill the hills of southeastern Nebraska near Peru, with the broad valley of the Missouri River far in the distance.*

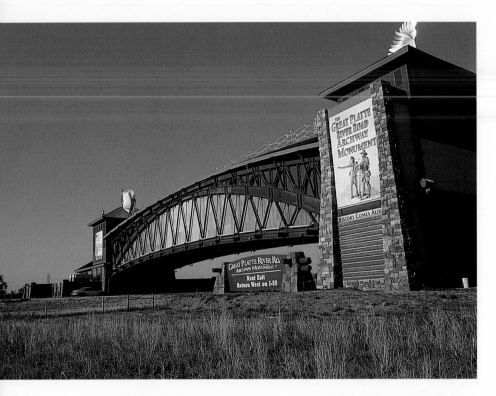

ABOVE: *The only structure to span Interstate 80 in Nebraska other than a bridge, the Great Platte River Road Archway Monument at Kearney is actually a museum. Its displays relate to those who have traveled the Platte River Valley over the years, including fur traders, those who ventured on the Oregon, California, and Mormon Pioneer Trails, early automobile enthusiasts, and today's motorists.*

RIGHT: *Created in 1964 on the Snake River southwest of Valentine, Merritt Reservoir has 44 miles of shoreline encompassing 2,900 surface acres of water. Although loved for its boating, swimming, fishing, and camping, the state recreation area surrounding the reservoir is also a favorite gathering spot for astronomers, who can gaze up at the heavens without the glare of the city lights. LARRY MAYER*

*Near Crossover Road in southern Sioux County, cattle congregate at tanks
filled with water pumped from underground sources by a windmill.*

ABOVE: A bronco rider prepares for his ride in North Platte's Buffalo Bill Arena during that city's NEBRASKAland Days. The annual event honors the first professional rodeo, which occurred here on July 4, 1882, and was created by William F. "Buffalo" Bill Cody, who lived in North Platte for more than 30 years.

RIGHT: Built in 1858, the First Presbyterian Church in Bellevue is now a historic site. Its congregation, organized in 1850 with only five members, now holds services in a more modern church about a mile away; the original structure is still a popular place for weddings.

ABOVE: *Water and land create an interplay of dark and light on a late summer day, Valentine National Wildlife Refuge.*

FACING PAGE: *The sharp slant of morning sunlight reveals the extent of the rolling rumpled hills and valleys in southern Washington County.*

ABOVE: Visitors stand at an overlook in the Lied Jungle at Henry Doorly Zoo. Rated by Reader's Digest as the best zoo in the nation and visited more than any other attraction in Nebraska, the Omaha zoo has the world's largest indoor jungle, indoor desert, and nocturnal exhibit.

FACING PAGE: Ponderosa pines stand scattered across the dry hills and valleys in Chadron State Park. Established in 1921, the state's oldest state park occupies 974 acres in the Pine Ridge, a 100-mile-long range of rugged limestone bluffs and buttes that arcs across the northwest corner of Nebraska.

LEFT: *The morning sun awakens flocks of sandhill cranes that have spent the night in the waters of the Platte River south of Kearney. More than half a million sandhill cranes—nearly 80 percent of their population in North America—visit the Platte each March on their northbound migration.*

BELOW: *The distinctive paint scheme of the Union Pacific Railroad brightens a mail car on display at North Platte's Cody Park Railroad Museum.*

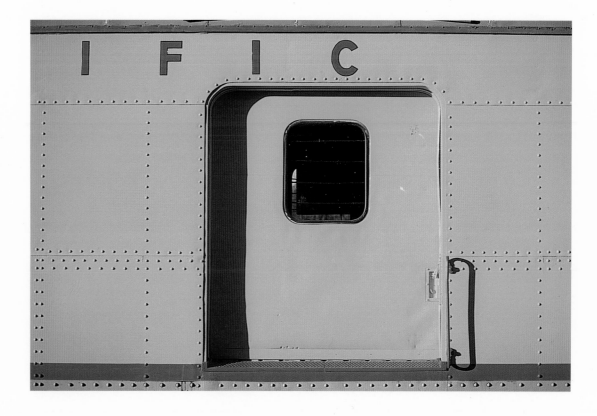

ABOVE: *Re-enactors portray soldiers from the 1820s at Fort Atkinson State Historical Park. Built in 1819 on a site recommended by Lewis and Clark years earlier, the fort had more than 1,100 soldiers, making it the nation's largest military outpost. In 1827, the Army abandoned the fort, which had been named after its first commander, Colonel Henry Atkinson.*

LEFT: *Overlooking Omaha's Gene Leahy Mall, the 40-story First National Tower is the tallest building between Chicago and Denver. Completed in 2002, the 633-foot-tall office building replaced the Woodman Building, built in 1967 and 485 feet tall, as the city's tallest building.*

ABOVE: *Weighing up to a ton, the bison is North America's heaviest animal. At one time, up to 60 million buffalo roamed North America. Now, about 350,000 bison remain in the U.S., with around 7,000 living in Nebraska, including these at Fort Niobrara National Wildlife Refuge.*

RIGHT: *Prairie grasses meet limestone bluffs and pines at Oglala National Grassland in the northwest corner of Nebraska. Covering 94,400 acres, Oglala National Grassland is the second largest tract of public land in Nebraska; only the 115,703-acre McKelvie National Forest is larger.*

RIGHT: *A great horned owl gives a steely stare from its perch in a tree at Swan Lake Wildlife Management Area.* MICHAEL FORSBERG

BELOW: *Rippled by the wind, miniature dunes lie among a sparse growth of prairie grasses in an exposed sandhill south of Wood Lake. When the topsoil of a sandhill is removed or erodes, a blowout results and the hill begins to move with the wind.*

FACING PAGE: *Bare branches of fallen cottonwoods appear to stretch menacingly in Fontenelle Forest in Bellevue.*

PREVIOUS PAGES: Rugged lands lie exposed to the weather and are bleached by the sun near Sand Creek in the southern part of the Oglala National Grassland.

LEFT: Lincoln's colorful Sunken Gardens have been a popular place since they were created on a small patch of ground at 27th Street and Capital Parkway in 1930. More than 110 types of annuals are planted here each year, in addition to non-native trees and plants such as banana trees, castor beans, and false tobacco.

BELOW: Sprays of water irrigate a farm field near Grand Island. Nebraska has more users and manufacturers of center-point irrigation systems than any other state.

A farmer works a field in the wide valley of the Republican River in Hitchcock County.

A land of rough limestone ridges and pine-filled canyons, the Pine Ridge is the most prominent geological feature in Sioux and Dawes Counties in northwest Nebraska. *LARRY MAYER*

ABOVE: *Morning light warms sandhill cranes wading in the Platte River near Kearney. Others have already taken to wing, heading for fields where they will fatten for the next leg of the journey to their northern nesting grounds.*

RIGHT: *The sun sets over the lush Knox County hills, which overlook the floodplain of the Missouri River, on the right.*

ABOVE: *Cattle graze on rolling hills in southern Stanton County.*

RIGHT: *One of the first great rocky landmarks seen by those who traveled west on the nearby Oregon Trail was Jail Rock, south of Bridgeport. Capped by very hard minerals, this rocky escarpment stands 400 feet above the base of the valley and has resisted erosion that has weathered away the surrounding terrain over the eons.*

PREVIOUS PAGES: *Coiling back upon itself time and again like a wandering snake, the North Loup River passes through the Sandhills east of Brewster as cattle graze upon its floodplain.*

LEFT: *Morning sunlight picks out details of the low-lying Sandhills on a fall day in Thomas County.*

RIGHT: *A sailing enthusiast takes his boat for a ride on Cunningham Lake, northwest of Omaha. Cunningham is one of several manmade lakes in the Omaha metro area that provide recreation as well as flood control on the Papio Creek and its tributaries.*

BELOW: *Waters of the Niobrara River (foreground) are about to meet those of the Missouri near Niobrara State Park.*

RIGHT AND BELOW: Among Nebraska's native animals are the prairie dog and one of its predators, the prairie rattlesnake. On September 7, 1804, the men of the Lewis and Clark Expedition became the first Americans to see a prairie dog, which they described as a "barking squirrel." After pouring five barrels of water down one hole in a rather large prairie dog town near today's Lynch, they finally succeeded in capturing one. They later sent it, still alive, to President Thomas Jefferson in Washington, D.C.

FACING PAGE: Trees still line Ash Hollow just as travelers on the Oregon Trail found them from 1840 to 1860 when they rested in the shade here and made this a major stop on their way west. Now a state historical park northwest of Ogallala, Ash Hollow still has ruts and other evidence of where thousands of wagons and people passed.

RIGHT: A trio of horses stands near a water tank and windmill in the Sandhills just east of Snake River Falls in Cherry County.

FACING PAGE: Slipping between the colors of fall, the shallow waters of the Niobrara River round a bend in the eastern part of the Fort Niobrara National Wildlife Refuge. In a region northeast of Valentine, the river valley forms a narrow corridor in the Sandhills where eastern and western ecosystems mesh, including northern boreal, ponderosa pine, and eastern deciduous forests and tallgrass, mixed-grass, and shortgrass prairies.

116

RIGHT: With small purple petals and a fine stamen, the Rocky Mountain bee plant grows where the topsoil has been disturbed, eroded, or removed in the Sandhills. The bee plant was a source of food for several Native American tribes; it was also used to alleviate stomachaches.

BELOW: Tubers take it easy on the Middle Loup River where it passes through the Bessey District of the Nebraska National Forest near Halsey.

FACING PAGE: Deer cross the Niobrara River near Valentine. Other mammals roaming freely along the Niobrara include coyotes, beavers, raccoons, squirrels, eastern cottontails, and minks. Because of its unique set of ecosystems, the valley is home to some animals rarely seen in other parts of Nebraska, such as olive-pocket mice, Bailey's eastern woodrats, southern bog lemmings, and Keen's and Brazilian free-tailed bats. LARRY MAYER

119

Near day's end, the sun casts warm colors upon the gently flowing waters of a stream in Morrill County.